THE GOLDEN BOOK
DUBLIN

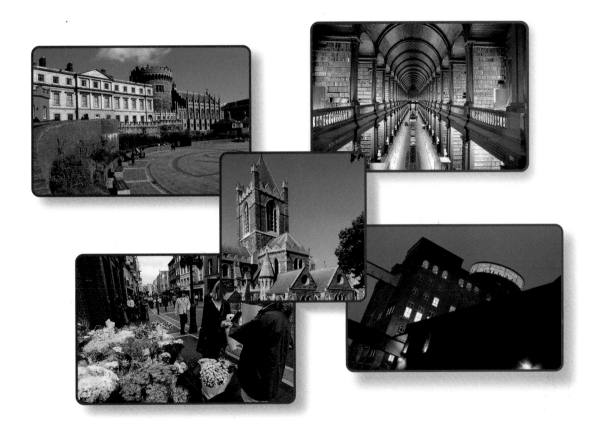

Text by
Betty Barrett *and* Frances Power

170 Colour illustrations

EB
BONECHI
O'BRIEN

CONTENTS

© Copyright by Casa Editrice Bonechi - Florence - Italy
Tel. +39 055576841 - Fax +39 0555000766 - e-mail: bonechi@bonechi.it - Internet: www.bonechi.it www.bonechi.com
ISBN 978-88-476-1271-6

Publication created by Casa Editrice Bonechi. Publication Manager: Monica Bonechi
Photographic research: Editorial Staff of Casa Editrice Bonechi
Graphic design, layout and cover: Manuela Ranfagni
Editing: Anna Baldini, Patrizia Fabbri, Susan Houlden
Maps and drawings: Stefano Benini
Texts by Betty Barrett and Frances Power

Printed in Italy by Centro Stampa Editoriale Bonechi.

PHOTOGRAPHY ACKNOWLEDGMENTS
Photographs from archives of Casa Editrice Bonechi taken by Ghigo Roli.
Credits:
(key: t=top; m=middle; b=bottom; a=all; l=left; r=right)
© Atlantide (Stefano Amantini): back cover (t r and b), pages 10, 13 (t), 14 (t), 19 (t), 26, 27 (t), 33 (b r), 34 (b), 39 (t r and b m), 43 (t), 46 (b), 47 (t); © Riccardo Bianchi:
page 55 (m both); © The Trustees of The Chester Beatty Library, Dublin: page 28 (b); © Maurizio Fraschetti: back cover (t l), pages 12 (b r), 42 (b);
© George Munday: pages 6 (b), 8 (t and b), 8-9 (b m), 9 (t and m), 14 (b r), 17 (l m), 21 (b r), 23 (b), 32 (b r), 33 (b l), 36 (m l), 37 (t r and m), 41 (t r and b l), 43 (b r), 44 (r),
46 (t), 47 (b), 50 (a), 53 (b r), 56 (b), 58 (both), 59 (b), 62 (b), 63 (b); © The National Gallery of Ireland: pages 16 (b), 17 (b r), also courtesy of the estate of Sir John Lavery;
© The National Museum of Ireland: pages 4 (t l), 8 (l m), 24 (t and b); © The O'Brien Press, photographs: Ian Broad, front cover (t r), pages 13 (m l), 31 (t r), 35 (b m), 36 (r),
45 (t), 49 (b), Peter Pearson, pages 21 (m), 23 (t r), Robert Vance, page 40 (b); © Oisin Gallery, artist Thomas Spelman, page 12 (t r), © St Patrick's Cathedral, page 35 (b l),
© Roger Stalley/Trinity College Department of History of Art, page 31 (m); © Lara Pessina: pages 3 (l), 11 (b); © Andrea Pistolesi: pages 18 (b), 25, 37 (b);
© Sandro Vannini: pages 7 (b), 17 (t r), 35 (b r), 59 (m).
Photos courtesy granted of:
Dublinia, Dublin: page 31 (b); Dublin City Council/David Meehan: page 30 (b r); Guinness Storehouse: pages 1 (b r), 7 (t), 29 (t and b m); The James Joyce Cultural
Museum: page 48 (t l); Emma Byrne © The O'Brien Press: front cover (l), back cover (b), pages 4-5 (b m), 5 (m r), 9 (b r), 13 (m r, b l and r), 16 (t), 17 (t l), 20,
21 (t r and b l), 23 (m l), 39 (t l and r), 41 (t l and b r), 44 (l), 48 (t), 49 (t), 55 (t and b), 60.

The publisher apologises for any omissions and is willing to make amends with the formal recognition of the author of any photo subsequently identified.

*   *   *

THE HISTORY OF DUBLIN

Dublin, as Ireland's capital city, is steeped in a long and colourful history. In 1988 the city celebrated its official millennium, but there is evidence that Dublin was inhabited as far back as 140AD when it was known as Eblana. The early Celtic settlement was Áth Cliath (Irish for 'hurdle ford', referring to a crossing at the River Liffey). The modern name for Dublin is Baile Átha Cliath ('town of the hurdle ford'). Dublin is the English name of the city. Saint Patrick is said to have visited Dublin in 448AD where he baptised converts to Christianity.

The real history of Dublin as a city begins in 841AD when the Vikings sailed up the River Liffey in their longboats. They established a trading post at Duib-linn, a 'black pool' formed where the River Poddle entered the River Liffey. The Vikings came from Scandinavia to plunder the thriving Irish monasteries of the 'Island of Saints and Scholars'. Some of these Viking invaders stayed in Dublin, married into native Irish families, adopted Christianity and opened Ireland up to trade with Europe. The Vikings were defeated by the High King Brian Boru in 1014 at the Battle of Clontarf, a few kilometres north of Dublin city. Another wave of invaders followed as the Normans, having conquered England in 1066, moved west into Ireland. In 1169 they arrived in Wexford, south of Dublin. Under the leadership of Richard FitzGilbert de Clare, also known as Strongbow, they established a centre of power in Dublin in 1170 and English rule in Ireland began. They too intermarried with the Irish and adopted their customs. Their power was largely confined to Dublin and a small area surrounding the city known as 'The Pale'. Outside The Pale, Ireland remained defiant of invaders.

The Normans were great castle- and church-builders, teaching the Irish to use stone instead of wood. Between 1173 and 1240 they rebuilt Christ Church Cathedral in Romanesque and Gothic style, and in 1190 they reconstructed St Patrick's Cathedral, located just outside the walls of the city on the oldest Christian site in Dublin. These magnificent cathedrals which you see today are symbols of medieval man's hope and salvation. In 1204 Dublin Castle was built by order of King John. It was to be the seat of British power in Ireland for seven hundred years.

Dublin's history in the following centuries was a series of misfortunes. In 1348 the Black Death, the greatest catastrophe in recorded history, gripped Dublin. In 1534 Silken Thomas FitzGerald failed in his rebellion against English rule. 1537 saw the dissolution of the monasteries by Henry VIII. In 1649 Oliver Cromwell turned his attention from the Civil War in England to rebellion in Ireland. He arrived in Ireland, took the city of Dublin, stabling his horses in St Patrick's Cathedral, and ruthlessly crushed the rebellion. By the end of the Cromwellian war the Irish population had fallen to about 500,000 as the result of the massacres, plague and famine. The Irish were driven off their properties and the lands granted to Protestant colonists. To repress the Irish Catholics, a new series of laws, the Penal Laws, were introduced.

Dublin Castle, dating from 1204.

The front square of Trinity College, founded in 1592.

An Irish parliament was set up in Dublin but this was an exclusively Protestant assembly.

Ireland backed the losing side in 1690 as William of Orange (Protestant) and James II (Catholic), two would-be English kings, struggled for control at the Battle of the Boyne. William was victorious, and James fled to France.

The period of the Protestant Ascendancy led Dublin into its 18th-century years of prosperity; it became the second city of the British Empire after London and the fifth largest city in Europe. When the Earl of Kildare built Leinster House (now the Irish Parliament) in the south of the city he forecast that fashion would follow him and sure enough the elegant homes on Merrion Square and Fitzwilliam Square were built close by. In 1757 the Wide Street Commissioners set about redesigning the streetscape of the city.

1796 saw the abortive French-backed invasion led by the Dublin Protestant Theobald Wolfe Tone. Another unsuccessful rebellion by the United Irishmen followed in 1798. Five years later, in 1803, Robert Emmet, also a young Dublin Protestant, led another unsuccessful revolt. Emmet was publicly executed and became one of the most famous Irish revolutionaries in the struggle for independence.

The Act of Union in 1801 created The United Kingdom of Great Britain and Ireland and ended the separate Irish parliament. As a result, Dublin's prosperity declined rapidly. In 1829 Daniel O'Connell succeeded in reclaiming basic rights for the Irish Catholics with the Act of Catholic Emancipation. He became known as 'The Liberator'.

A terrible national disaster struck with the Great Famine of 1845-1851, reducing the population from 8 million to 6.6 million through starvation, disease and emigration. The Famine heralded a desperate national decline. By 1911 Ireland's population had fallen to 4.4 million. Emigration created another Ireland abroad in Britain and America. In 1858 the Irish in America were instrumental in founding, in Dublin, the secret revolutionary society of the Fenian Brotherhood, from which grew the Irish Republican Army (IRA). Nationalist movements continued to grow during the 19th and 20th centuries. 1905 saw the formation of the republi-

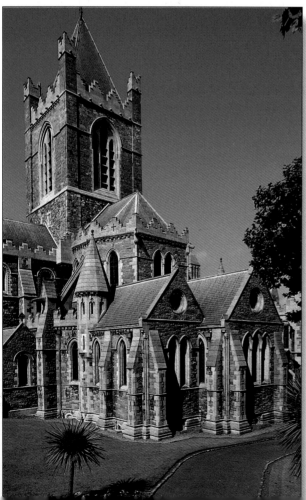

Top left, the 8th-century Tara Brooch in the National Museum, bottom left, Christ Church Cathedral, founded originally in 1037.

can movement Sinn Féin, 'Ourselves Alone'. Charles Stewart Parnell (1846-1891), known as 'The Uncrowned King of Ireland', campaigned tirelessly for Home Rule and Irish land reform. The Home Rule Bill was finally passed in 1912 but failed to be implemented due to the outbreak of World War I, which resulted in the loss of 50,000 Irish soldiers.

The major uprising against the British occurred at Easter in April 1916. A group of Irish Volunteers marched on the General Post Office (GPO) on O'Connell Street, the Irish flag was raised over the building and outside Patrick Pearse read the Proclamation from the Provisional Government of the Irish Republic to the people of Ireland. Other key points in the city were secured by the rebels. The British Army moved into action and the Irish forces were soon outnumbered. Patrick Pearse agreed to an unconditional ceasefire. This rising had limited support but the execution of the leaders transformed them into national heroes and the cry for a free Ireland grew louder.

The general election of 1918 resulted in success for 73 Sinn Féin candidates; they refused to take their seats in London. The first independent Irish parliament, called the 'Assembly of Ireland' or Dáil Éireann, held its first session in 1919. Several members were absent due to their imprisonment. The British authorities did everything in their power to bring down this threat to British rule. At the same time, the Irish Republican Army (IRA) began their terrorist strikes against symbols of British control. This violent War of Independence lasted until a truce was signed in 1921, followed by the Anglo-Irish Treaty, creating the Irish Free State, but minus the six north-eastern counties. The Northern Ireland question remains unsolved to this day.

Civil War broke out in 1922 between the anti-Treaty forces and the pro-Treaty forces. In the same year, Michael Collins, the charismatic military commander of the pro-Treaty forces met his death in an ambush in County Cork. The Civil War drew to a close in 1923, leaving 4,000 dead. The fight for independence and the Civil War took their toll on

Dublin's streets and many important buildings were destroyed or scarred by the fighting.

In 1932 Eamon de Valera, leading the Fianna Fáil political party, won the general election and proceeded to draw up the Irish Constitution in 1937. The government declared the Free State a Republic in 1948.

The entry of the Republic into the European Economic Community in 1973 brought benefits to agriculture, infrastructure and tourism. Ireland witnessed an economic boom in the 1990s, largely due to the young, well-educated population. This attracted multinational companies in pharmaceuticals and information technology to Dublin, and to Ireland. In the mid-1990s, the International Financial Services Centre turned Dublin into an important hub for European banking and investment services. All of these factors led to unemployment and emigration falling to an all-time low. Alongside this period of economic growth, a new awareness of the city's architecture developed and great efforts have been made to restore and improve Dublin's streets and buildings. Today Dublin is an evolving, thriving and energetic city.

Top, *Georgian Dublin*, middle, *the Ha'penny Bridge*, bottom left, *the Custom House*.

A CITY BETWEEN THE MOUNTAINS AND THE SEA

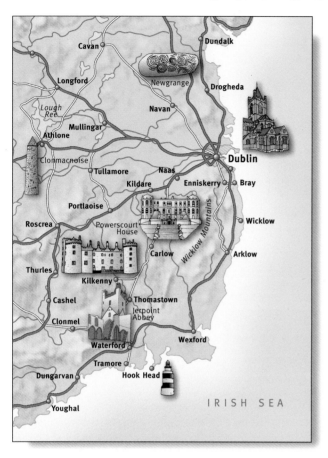

ublin lies on the east coast of Ireland, nestling between the Irish Sea and the Dublin/Wicklow Mountains. Dublin Bay sweeps from north to south in a horseshoe shape with the capital in the centre. To the south of the bay is the charming coastal village of Dalkey, with fine views from the headland. To the north of the bay is Howth, a fishing village and marina. From the west flows the River Liffey, in from the plains of County Kildare and out into the Irish Sea. The river is the spiritual heart of Dublin, dividing the city into north and south. To explore Dublin Bay you can take a DART train (Dublin Area Rapid Transport), an overground electrical train that provides a frequent and efficient service to the north and south of the city centre. Dublin weather is something like the Dublin people – unpredictable but never dull for long. There is an Irish saying: 'If you don't like the weather in Ireland, wait five minutes.' The warm currents of the Gulf Stream guarantee mild winters with average temperatures of 4–8°C and cool summers with average temperature of 14–16°C. It is always wise to bring a rain jacket; the average annual rainfall in the Dublin area is approximately 700 millimetres, but it seldom snows.

A panoramic view of Dublin Bay.

DUBLIN TODAY

Top, *the Gravity Bar at the Guinness Storehouse*, bottom, *one of the best ways to see the main sights, by open-top bus.*

In recent years Dublin has experienced a vibrant revival. Ireland's largest and most cosmopolitan city welcomes 4.5 million visitors each year. Alongside the decorative Georgian architecture, the many pubs, the literary and historical traditions and the ever-present sound of music, one of the most striking aspects of the capital today is the huge number of young people. The population of Dublin is 1.2 million, with 40% under the age of twenty-five. Dublin is a city for people-watching, for the talk and for walking. Two of the best ways to see the city are a walking tour or a hop-on-hop-off, open-top bus tour.

The elegant splendour of 18th-century Georgian Dublin is to be found in Merrion and Fitzwilliam squares. The magnificent 12th-century cathedrals of St Patrick's and Christ Church stand within easy reach of each other. Dublin is a city of contrasts: a touching sculpture of starving famine victims setting out for the emigrant ship on Custom House Quay stands across the road from the prosperous Irish Financial Services Centre.

History is absorbed in the bullet-scarred General Post Office (GPO) on O'Connell Street, in the cold metal doors of Kilmainham Gaol and in the cobblestones of Trinity College. There, in the Old Library, lies the famous Book of Kells, a stunning 1,300-year-old illustrated manuscript, declared by some the most beautiful book in the world.

On a guided tour of Dublin Castle you will see Waterford crystal chandeliers, Donegal wool carpets and hear the echoes of Irish history. Within the grounds of the castle the Chester Beatty Library displays rare Eastern manuscripts, prints, icons, fine art from the great cultures and religions of the world.

A short stroll outside the walls of Trinity College takes the visitor to Nassau Street with its wide range of stores for Irish crystal, traditional knitwear and music, pottery and linen. Around the corner from Nassau Street, shoppers throng Grafton Street, a pedestrianised smart shopping area. Undergoing a revival,

Henry Street to the north, with its nearby thriving Moore Street market, offers more to the shopper.

Dublin is perhaps most famous for its pub life and there are 750 pubs to choose from for that leisurely pint of Guinness ('just because it's good for you'). At the Guinness Storehouse you can learn about the famous stout that has been brewed in the city for 250 years and sink a 'pint of plain' in the Gravity Bar with its spectacular view of the city. At the Old Jameson Distillery you can qualify as an Irish whiskey taster!

The Temple Bar area comes alive at night with a huge selection of restaurants, pubs and nightclubs. During the day you can browse the trendy shops, book and food markets and linger at street performances and open-air concerts.

Dublin is, of course, renowned as a city of writers. At the Dublin Writers' Museum you can discover more about the three Dublin-born Irish winners of the Nobel Prize for Literature, WB Yeats, Samuel Beckett and George Bernard Shaw, among many other literary greats. The Literary Pub Crawl, which departs from The Duke Pub on Duke Street, is an entertaining way to learn about Irish literature. The show features professional actors who perform works from great Irish writers while visiting Dublin's best-known literary pubs. The James Joyce Cultural Centre is located in the north of the city and the James Joyce Museum is a short trip south of the city centre, to a Martello Tower at Sandycove. Dublin is also proud of its rich theatrical tradition and boasts many theatres. The Abbey is the national theatre with productions by Irish playwrights such as Seán O'Casey, Tom Murphy, Hugh Leonard and Brian Friel. Music lies at the soul of the city from large venues such as The National Concert Hall to the more intimate pub scene. Irish traditional music has experienced a huge revival and can be heard in some

Top, Bloomsday, 16 June, when the city celebrates James Joyce's Ulysses, middle, WB Yeats, Dublin-born winner of the Nobel Prize for Literature, bottom, Oscar Wilde's statue Merrion Square.

pubs in the evening. Best known are O'Donoghue's on Merrion Row and the Brazen Head on Bridge Street, which is Dublin's oldest pub, established in 1198. Johnnie Fox's pub in the Wicklow Mountains, just south of the city, claims to be the highest pub in Ireland and is known for its 'hooley nights'. Dublin's rock and modern music scene has always been alive with new and upcoming bands, and in recent years the city has nurtured such worldwide talents as U2 and The Frames.

The National Gallery on Merrion Square is home to the famous Caravaggio painting, 'The Taking of Christ'. The Gallery also houses works by many Irish artists, including Jack B. Yeats, William Orpen and Sir John Lavery. Close by in Kildare Street is the National Museum, displaying such treasures as the Ardagh Chalice and the Tara Brooch. Also in this area the following galleries have exhibitions of contemporary Irish artists: The Frederick, the Hallward and the Oriel galleries. The Hugh Lane Gallery in the north of the city houses the Francis Bacon studio. A bus ride west of the centre takes you to the Royal Hospital Kilmainham, home of the Irish Museum of Modern Art. For those looking for peace and quiet there are two public parks in the centre of the city: St Stephen's Green and Merrion Square. In Merrion Square the intriguing, multi-coloured statue of Oscar Wilde looks across to the house where he grew up. The large Phoenix Park in the north-west of the city is home to Dublin's Zoo with its wonderful African Plains. To enjoy the River Liffey, and some of the city's finest buildings, take a stroll along the boardwalk.

The *Irish Times*, the premier daily newspaper, has a column entitled 'What's On' which details the latest events, and the Dublin Tourism Centre on Suffolk Street will supply all the information you need for a great stay in Dublin.

Top, *traditional Irish music is popular in Dublin pubs,*
middle, *the Spire, O'Connell Street,* bottom, *Merchant's Arch,*
a pedestrian route from Temple Bar to the Ha'penny Bridge,
bottom left, *the Millennium Bridge.*

Trinity College

Trinity College is the oldest university in the country and was founded in 1592 by Queen Elizabeth I of England on the confiscated grounds of the former Priory of All Hallows. Up until then the Protestant Anglo-Irish ruling class had been sending their sons to the Continent to be educated where they ran the risk of becoming 'infected with Popery'. Trinity was to become the centre of Protestant education and for 250 years was the only university in Ireland. It continued to be used mainly by the Protestant population until the second half of this century – until 1966 Catholics who studied at Trinity had to obtain a special dispensation from their archbishop or risk excommunication. By 1990, however, roughly 75 per cent of the 8,000 students at Trinity were Catholic.

The college sits at the heart of Dublin. Its 90-metre curved façade ends a long vista down Dame Street, one of the city's main thoroughfares. While none of the original 16th-century buildings now survives, the campus provides a fascinating guide to the work of many important architects over the centuries. The restrained façade, which acts as a balance to the exuberance of the Bank of Ireland building opposite, was designed by Theodore Jacobsen in the mid-18th-century.

Behind its façade lie a number of interconnecting cobbled quadrangles surrounded by mainly 18th-century buildings with some Victorian and 20th-century additions.

The first and largest of the quadrangles is **Front Square** or **Parliament Square** (the building costs were met by Parliament). On either side of Front Square two wings of student residences ensure that Trinity plays a lively part in Dublin social and cultural life. Beyond the residences and set back a little from Front Square are two matched porticos – on the right the **Exam Hall** and on the left the **Chapel**, with splendid plasterwork by Michael Stapleton – both designed in the classical style by the Scottish architect Sir William Chambers. They were built in the 1780s, and are the last Georgian additions to the college. Beside the Chapel stands the **Dining Hall**, designed in the 1740s by the German architect Richard Cassells who is responsible for much of Georgian Dublin. Destroyed by fire in 1984, it has since been beautifully refurbished and the adjoining building, the **Atrium,** has been hollowed out to form a three storey-high performance space, which is overlooked by wooden galleries.

In the centre of Front Square the Victorian baroque

Trinity College is the oldest university in Ireland, established in 1592 by Queen Elizabeth I.

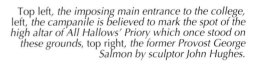

Top left, *the imposing main entrance to the college,* left, *the campanile is believed to mark the spot of the high altar of All Hallows' Priory which once stood on these grounds,* top right, *the former Provost George Salmon by sculptor John Hughes.*

campanile, donated by the Archbishop of Armagh in 1853, is believed to stand on the spot once occupied by the high altar of the Priory of All Hallows. During students' ragweek, the campanile is often decorated with bicycles and other unexpected ornaments.

The **Rubrics**, the red-brick student residences which stand directly behind the campanile, are the oldest set of buildings in the college, dating back to 1701 and the reign of Queen Anne, but even these were re-vamped in the Victorian period. Richard Cassells also contributed the **Printing House**, a miniature Doric temple and an architectural gem, which stands in **New Square** behind the Rubrics. Completed in 1734, it was his earliest Dublin work. Another building worth noting in the same square is the **Museum Building**, designed in the Venetian Gothic style in 1852 by Sir Thomas Deane and Benjamin Woodward. It was to influence the work of architects for the remainder of the century. Outside, are wonderful stone carvings of animals, fruit and flowers, while the grand marble interior is home to a skeleton of the giant Irish Elk. Deane and Woodward also enlarged **Trinity Library**, designed by Thomas Burgh in 1792.

Modern buildings such as the **Arts Block**, a library and lecture hall complex, and the **Berkeley Library**, with its massive concrete and granite façade, both designed

by Ahrends, Burton and Koralek, were added in the 1970s and 1980s and enclose the remaining sides of the square formed by Burgh's Library. 2003 saw the opening of the state-of-the-art **Ussher Library**. Overlooking the **Sports Field**, the Samuel Beckett Theatre Centre, a wooden structure on stilts, designed by Dublin architects de Blacam and Meagher in the 1990s, houses two theatres for student and experimental work.

Many interesting sculptural works both modern and classical populate the campus. Those outside the front of Trinity commemorate two well-known *alumni*, philosopher and orator Edmund Burke (1729-97) and Oliver Goldsmith (1728-74), author of *She Stoops to Conquer* and *The Vicar of Wakefield.* Many other noted Anglo-Irish figures studied at Trinity including the satirist Jonathan Swift (1667-1745), patriot Wolfe Tone (1763-98), Oscar Wilde (1854-1900), JM Synge (1871-1909) whose *Playboy of the Western World* caused riots when first shown at the Abbey Theatre, and Nobel Prizewinner Samuel Beckett (1906-89).

Samuel Beckett (1906–1989)

Samuel Beckett, novelist, dramatist and poet, was born in the fashionable suburb of Foxrock, south County Dublin. In 1923 Beckett entered Trinity College. For most of his life he lived in France. His most famous play, *Waiting for Godot,* was produced in Dublin in 1955.
In 1969 Beckett was awarded the Nobel Prize for Literature.
He died in Paris.

Top, *the college grounds are full of sculpture, both classical and modern such as* 'Sphere with Sphere', *by Arnaldo Pomodoro. Bottom left, the Long Room of Trinity College Library, and,* bottom right, *a detail from the 8th-century illuminated manuscript known as* The Book of Kells.

Trinity Library

Designed in 1792 by Thomas Burgh, **Trinity Library** contains the famous **Long Room** which at 64 metres by 12.2 metres is the largest single chamber library in Europe. In 1859, Sir Thomas Deane and Benjamin Woodward added a barrel-vaulted ceiling, which gives the library both much needed extra space and a lofty elegance. Best known of the library's treasures is *The Book of Kells*, an 8th-century manuscript of the four gospels produced in the *scriptorium* of the monastery at Kells in County Meath and on Iona off the coast of Scotland. Many Irish monasteries had *scriptoria* attached where scribes laboured over pre-Christian legends, epics and histories as well as the scriptures. In the margins they often jotted down poems of praise or complaint – some of them very witty. It is thanks to these scribes – and the missionaries who went to the Continent during the Dark Ages – that Ireland earned itself the name of the 'Land of Saints and Scholars'. These illuminated manuscripts were highly prized and so always under threat of theft – a few pages at the front and back of *The Book of Kells* have been lost, perhaps when the book was stolen from Kells in 1006 and stripped of its gold cover.

The Bank of Ireland

The imposing **Bank of Ireland** on College Green was formerly Parliament House, designed by Edward Lovett Pearce in 1729, and is the city's most noble Palladian building. The Corinthian portico on Westmoreland Street, designed by James Gandon, was added in 1785 to provide the House of Lords with its own entrance. The last parliament sat here in January 1801 and the Bank of Ireland purchased the building in 1803.

Top, *the monumental façade of the Bank of Ireland, with its colonnaded forecourt, faces south across College Green.*

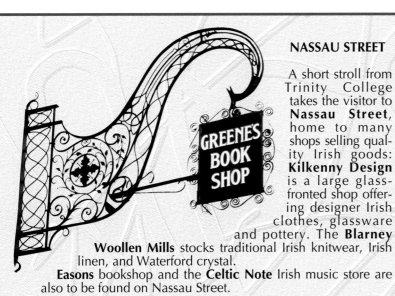

NASSAU STREET

A short stroll from Trinity College takes the visitor to **Nassau Street**, home to many shops selling quality Irish goods: **Kilkenny Design** is a large glass-fronted shop offering designer Irish clothes, glassware and pottery. The **Blarney Woollen Mills** stocks traditional Irish knitwear, Irish linen, and Waterford crystal.

Easons bookshop and the **Celtic Note** Irish music store are also to be found on Nassau Street.

Traditional Dublin shops.

Leinster House

Top left, *Victorian cast-iron work hides the fact that the Mansion House dates from 1710,* above, *Department of the Taoiseach, the Irish Prime Minister,* and, top right, *Leinster House, seat of government.*

Mansion House

Home to Dublin's lord mayors since 1715. Although the exterior has been reworked with Victorian details, the house is one of the oldest in the area, dating from 1710. The interior still shows its Queen Anne origins.

Leinster House

The seat of Ireland's parliament, or *Dáil Éireann*, is **Leinster House**, built in 1745 for the Earl of Kildare in the days when fashionable folk lived on the north side of the Liffey. 'Wherever I go,' the Earl is supposed to have said, 'they will follow.' And he was right, the green fields which surrounded him where quickly developed into **Merrion Square**.

The Royal Dublin Society owned Leinster House from 1814 until the Irish government purchased it in 1925.

The National Library

The **National Library** on Kildare Street was once the library of the Royal Dublin Society (RDS), an institution committed to promoting advances in science, agriculture and the arts. Together with the **National Museum**, which faces it across the lawn of **Leinster House**, the two seats of education were envisaged as providing a cultural centre for Dubliners. The library building was designed by Sir Thomas Deane in 1890. Thousands of books, magazines, newspapers, maps and manuscripts relating to Ireland, including those collected by the RDS, are lodged here. The library also has a significant collection of first editions and preserves the manuscripts of leading Irish authors, complete with revisions, margin notes and doodles. The circular **Reading Room** is a delight to work in – as many of Ireland's finest modern writers have discovered. In fact, James Joyce, who frequented the library himself, sited the great literary debate in *Ulysses* here.

For anyone wishing to trace their roots, the National Library offers a **Genealogical Service** and the **Heraldic Museum**, 2-3 Kildare Street, displays the banners, shields and other heraldic insignia of well known Irish surnames.

Top and bottom, *views of the rotunda of the National Library on Kildare Street from outside and from within.*

National Gallery

First opened in 1864, the **National Gallery** now houses a collection of some 2,500 paintings and 10,000 other works of art, spanning from the 14th to the 20th centuries. All the major European Schools are represented.

There are two entrances to the gallery: the entrance from Clare Street, which leads to the **Millennium Wing**, and the old entrance on Merrion Square. The gallery consists of four wings on four levels.

The **Millennium Wing** houses a permanent exhibition of 20th-century Irish art, including paintings by William Leech, Sir John Lavery, William Orpen, and Louis le Brocquy. Visiting exhibitions take place in this wing and the restaurant, café and shop are to be found here.

In the **Dargan Wing**, on the ground floor, the **Shaw Room** displays a large canvas by Daniel Maclise, 'The Marriage of Strongbow and Aoife', and the **Yeats' Museum** presents work by Jack B. Yeats, brother of WB Yeats. Level two of the Dargan Wing shows 17th- and 18th-century Italian, Spanish, French and Flemish art.

The **Milltown Wing** is the central wing. On level one, among the 18th- and 19th-century Irish artists' work hang fine examples by the gifted landscape painters,

The National Gallery of Ireland.

'The Marriage of Strongbow and Aoife' (1847) by Daniel Maclise, in the Shaw Room.

Top left, *exterior of the Millennium Wing, at the National Gallery of Ireland,* top right, *inside of the Millennium Wing,* left, *a view of the interior of the gallery,* bottom, *Sir John Lavery's 'The Artist's Studio'.*

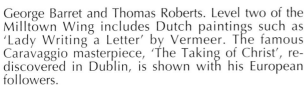

George Barret and Thomas Roberts. Level two of the Milltown Wing includes Dutch paintings such as 'Lady Writing a Letter' by Vermeer. The famous Caravaggio masterpiece, 'The Taking of Christ', re-discovered in Dublin, is shown with his European followers.

The **Beit Wing** is home to British and American art on level one and the **Print Gallery** on the mezzanine level. Paintings from the Italian Renaissance are located on level two.

There is no admission charge to the Gallery, except for visiting exhibitions.

Top, *buskers on Grafton Street, one of Dublin's busiest shopping streets, left, statue of Molly Malone.*

Grafton Street

Dublin's smartest shopping street bustles with shoppers, buskers and flower sellers. The many Victorian pubs, such as **McDaids**, in the side streets, offer a chance to sit and watch the crowds go by. The street is also home to the elegant store of **Brown Thomas** and many high-street shops such as **Marks & Spencers**. Down the intriguing Clarendon Street is the **Powerscourt Townhouse Shopping Centre** with its craft and designer shops, restaurants and stylish interior. A southside post office is to be found on South Anne Street, another side street. On nearby Dawson Street the visitor will discover two fine bookstores: **Hodges Figgis** and **Waterstones**.

Top, *Powerscourt Townhouse Shopping Centre.*

Right, *shoppers relax outside a famous Victorian pub.*

Bottom, *flower sellers on Grafton Street.*

St Stephen's Green

Until the philanthropist Lord Ardilaun, Sir Arthur Guinness, tidied up **St Stephen's Green** in 1880 and gave it to the public, the park had been leased to the house-owners around the square.

Sadly, most of these original houses fell victim to building developers in the 1960s, but the survivors are fine examples of the best townhouses of Georgian Dublin. On the south side at Nos 85-86 is **Newman House**, beautifully restored to its 18th century splendour. No 85 was designed by Richard Cassells in 1738 and contains unique plasterwork executed by the famous Italian stuccodores, the La Francini brothers. In the 19th century, Newman House became the home of University College Dublin (UCD), the Catholic alternative to Trinity College, where the English poet Gerard Manley Hopkins lectured until he died of typhoid in 1889. Shortly after Hopkins's death James Joyce became a student here – and he immortalised the experience in *A Portrait of the Artist as a Young Man.*

In the 1960s UCD moved out to the suburbs at the instigation of the Catholic Archbishop of Dublin who feared that students might be contaminated by their proximity to the Protestant college of Trinity. Beside No 85 is **University Church**, its plain exterior hiding a Byzantine fantasy inside. On the north side of the square, the gentlemen's clubs which lead up to the **Shelbourne Hotel** are a reminder of the days when St Stephen's Green was an exclusive address. Just as Lord Ardilaun intended, St Stephen's Green has become a popular park and Dubliners love to sunbathe, picnic or feed the ducks and swans who flock here.

Dotted all around the park are bandstands, benches, formal flowerbeds, statues – Joyce stands opposite his old college – and ornamental lakes. There is also a garden for the blind with scented plants labelled in braille.

Top and bottom, *views of St Stephen's Green, with the lake and a fountain.* Top right, *the Shelbourne Hotel, dating from 1824.* Right middle, *Newman House, the first Catholic University in Ireland, is located at Nos 85 and 86 St Stephen's Green. These fine Georgian buildings contain wonderful plasterwork by the La Francini brothers and Robert West.*

Right bottom, *commissioned by Cardinal Newman in 1856, University Church is Byzantine in character and stunningly decorated with four different kinds of Irish marble.*

Merrion Square, an oasis of calm.

Merrion Square

Dublin is famous for its elegant Georgian streetscapes and one of the best preserved is **Merrion Square**, which was built in the 1760s on land belonging to Lord Fitzwilliam. The Georgian townhouses may appear uniform, but each differs in its details – the doors, delicate fanlights, brass doorknockers, cast-iron foot scrapers and balconies. The north side of Merrion Square was the first to be built and was the fashionable side for the rich and famous to promenade. The houses on this side have rusticated granite up to the first-floor level and in the 19th century wrought-iron balconies were added. On the west side of Merrion Square is the **Rutland Fountain**, designed as a drinking fountain in 1791 and recently renovated. The large building, with the distinctive portico, opposite the fountain is the **National Gallery**. Next door is the 18th-century, Palladian building of **Leinster House**, today's government buildings.

In the 19th and early 20th centuries the townhouses were occupied by notable artists, politicians and writers. The many wall plaques bear witness to these residents, including WB Yeats, that magical, mystical poet and winner of the Nobel Prize for Literature, who lived at **No 82** from 1922-25, and Daniel O'Connell, known as the 'The Liberator' for his fight for Catholic emancipation in 1829, who occupied **No 58**. The writer and painter George W. Russell (AE) (1867-1935) lived at **No 84** and Sir William Wilde (1815-76), the famous eye-surgeon and father of Oscar Wilde, together with his wife, the poet 'Speranza', resided at **No 1** Merrion Square, which is now occupied by the American College. The square surrounds a delightful **park** – an oasis of calm and beauty. Designed as a private park for the residents of Merrion Square, it was purchased by the Archbishop of Dublin in 1930 as a site for a Catholic cathedral. This project was eventually abandoned and in 1974 the park was opened to the public by Dublin Corporation. Today this park has a children's playground, a bog garden, an interesting collection of old street lamps and statues of famous Irish figures such as Michael Collins, Irish statesman and hero of the War of Independence, who was killed during the Civil War in 1922 and Oscar Wilde, poet, wit, novelist and dramatist (1854-1900). The park plays host to open-air events during the summer months and is the perfect spot for a city picnic.

Top and right middle, *decorative details from Georgian houses in Merrion Square*, below, *Oscar Wilde statue*, bottom right, *inside No 29 Lower Fitzwilliam Street.*

Fitzwilliam Street

Fitzwilliam Street, which runs from **Leeson Street** down to **Holles Street Hospital** was once Europe's longest Georgian street. Many of Dublin's 18th-century houses are now offices but **No 29 Lower Fitzwilliam Street** has preserved the elegance of the Georgian era.

Top, the 8ᵗʰ-century Ardagh Chalice, and left, the 9ᵗʰ-century Ballinderry Viking Sword from the National Museum.

National Museum

Opened in 1890, the **National Museum of Ireland**, Kildare Street, contains artefacts dating from 2000BC to the 20ᵗʰ century. The great entrance hall with its vast rotunda leads to the **Pre-historic Ireland** exhibition, which displays the archaeological riches of the Stone and Bronze Ages. The next exhibition is **Ór**, Ireland's 'Gold', focusing on Europe's finest collection of Bronze Age gold ornaments. The **Treasury** features masterpieces of Celtic and medieval art such as the Broighter Hoard, the Ardagh Chalice and the Tara Brooch. The exhibition highlights the golden age of Irish art, which followed the introduction of Christianity to Ireland in the fifth century. Located close to the museum restaurant is the exhibition **The Road to Independence**, concerning the events and personalities of 1920-21 and the Easter Rising of 1916.

On the first floor, **Viking Age Ireland** concentrates on Irish archaeology from 795AD to approximately 1200AD, paying particular attention to the Viking settlement of Dublin. Also on the first floor the **Ancient Egypt** exhibition introduces the visitor to Egyptian civilisation. For the complete museum experience, the visitor can take the **Museumlink** bus to the **National Museum of Ireland**, **Collins Barracks**, Benburb Street, near the Phoenix Park, north of the Liffey. This building houses the decorative arts and focuses on the social, economic, political and military history of Ireland.

Natural History Museum

Dr David Livingstone opened the **Natural History Museum**, on Upper Merrion Street, in 1857, and this intriguing Victorian museum continues to draw many visitors every year. The **Irish Room** on the ground floor is largely devoted to Irish mammals, insects and sea creatures. Three skeletons of the giant Irish deer (which lived during the Ice Age), along with a myriad variety of birds and animals, are on display. This is the art of taxidermy at its finest. Some of these creatures are simply beautiful; others are small and fascinating in their detail. The **World Collection** on the first floor features mammals from Africa, Asia and Australia, including the enormous whale suspended from the roof, the extinct dodo and the giant panda. The upper floor is home to exotic insects such as leeches and spiders.

Some of the many exhibits inside the Natural History Museum.

Dublin Castle

Dublin Castle comes as a surprise – it no longer looks like a castle (only the **Record Tower** survives from its days as a fortified structure, and even its castellations are 19ᵗʰ-century additions). It is a hotch-potch of architectural styles, part modern, part medieval, but most of its buildings date from the elegant Dublin of the 18ᵗʰ century, and are grouped around an **Upper** and **Lower Yard**. For over 700 years there was no greater symbol of British power in Ireland than 'the Castle' and virtually every rebellion against the English aimed to overthrow it. None succeeded.

Built in 1204 on high ground to the south of the Liffey, the castle was originally bound on three sides by the Poddle river. Just below the castle walls the Poddle ran into a pool, the Black Pool or '*Dubh Linn*' after which the city is named. Remains of a Viking fort, *circa* 9ᵗʰ century, found during excavations in 1990, indicate that the site had always been of strategic importance and it is believed that an earlier rath existed here.

Originally, a sturdy tower guarded each corner of the curtain walls around a quadrangle roughly corresponding to the present Upper Yard, while the portcullis was at the centre of the **North Gate**. By 1242 a chapel had been built and fitted with stained-glass windows. A spacious hall where **St Patrick's Hall** now stands had been built and rebuilt by 1320. This original castle must have inspired respect – not only were rebels regularly decapitated and their heads used to decorate the castle walls, but there was the luxury of piped water.

For the first few centuries of British rule the castle was a constant target of attack during Irish rebellions. Silken Thomas, son of the Earl of Kildare, besieged the castle with cannons in 1534. Unfortunately for him, the city's officials were sitting inside the impregnable

The Upper Yard of Dublin Castle, showing the Bedford Tower which encloses the old west tower of the gate-house. It was from here that the Irish crown jewels were stolen in 1907 – and never seen again.

Dublin Castle is a mix of architectural periods, top, the Record Tower, dating from 1207, with on one side 18th-century buildings and on the other the Gothic Revival chapel by Francis Johnston, left, an ornate mirror in the Picture Gallery.

walls with large stocks of food and gunpowder. Not only was Silken Thomas captured, but he and five of his uncles were hung. In 1684 a fire devastated the residential quarters of the castle. They were rebuilt with a greater awareness of the castle's administrative functions – additional reception rooms and offices were included and the **Upper** and **Lower Yards** became recognisable in their present form.

But the castle still acted as the military centre and prison for the city. For three years, 15-year-old Hugh O'Donnell was held hostage in the **Record Tower** to ensure the good behaviour of his Ulster clan – a common English practice. On Christmas Eve 1592, he and some companions escaped, dressed only in fine linens and sandals. It was a freezing night with blizzards and howling gales and their journey took them on foot over the Wicklow mountains to Glenmalure. Hugh O'Donnell survived to be extolled by Irish *filí* or bards, but his companions died of exposure.

Rebuilding continued throughout the 18th century as the castle's role again altered. As the residence of the Viceroy, the representative of English power in Ireland, it became the epicentre of Anglo-Irish society, hosting balls and levées and entertaining visiting dignatories. Sir William Robinson who had designed the Royal Hospital Kilmainham carried out much of the work, while Sir Edward Lovett Pearce redecorated **St Patrick's Hall**. Much of the Georgian **Upper Yard** with the **Castle Hall**, simple and elegant in red brick, dates from this period, and for the hundred years from the end of the 18th century onwards, additions, reconstructions and amendments were constant.

In 1798 the British quashed another rebellion. It was a particularly bloody episode, with rebel corpses being laid out in the castle yard as trophies. One corpse was seen to move and, after being resuscitated, was granted a pardon but, as one observer commented, the rebel 'did not, however, change his principles'. By 1814 the **Chapel Royal**, now called the **Church of the Most Holy Trinity**, adjoining the **Record Tower,** had been designed in the Gothic Revival style by Francis Johnston. Inside are the coat of arms of every viceroy since the 12th century, with elaborate fan vaulting

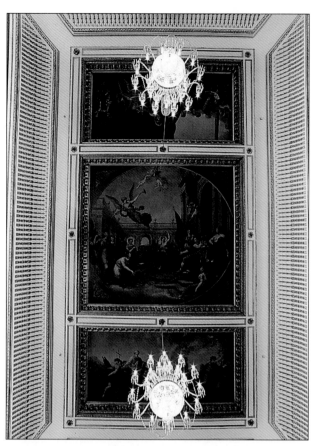

Top left, *interior of the Church of the Most Holy Trinity with exuberant plasterwork by Michael Stapleton,* top right, *18ᵗʰ-century painted panels in the ceiling of St Patrick's Hall.*
Bottom right, *'Ying Ying pines for her lover', by Zhang, late 17ᵗʰ century, taste of the Orient from the Chester Beatty Library and Museum.*

and plasterwork by stuccodore Michael Stapleton. Outside, Edward Smyth, known for his work on the Custom House and Four Courts, carved over a hundred stone heads of mythological and historical figures. The chapel was immediately proclaimed 'the most beautiful specimen of the Gothic style of Architecture in Europe'.

During the Rising of 1916, the castle was attacked once more, again without success. The castle was finally handed over to the Irish State in 1922 and now houses government offices.

The Chester Beatty Library and Gallery

In the **Clock Tower Building**, in the gardens of Dublin Castle, the **Chester Beatty Library and Gallery** opens windows on artistic treasures from Asia, the Middle East, North Africa and Europe. This collection of 22,000 manuscripts, rare books and beautiful objects was assembled by Sir Alfred Chester Beatty. An Eastern theme provides the ambience in the **Silk Road Café**.

Guinness Storehouse

Emigrants sigh for it, songs extol its virtues, nursing mothers were encouraged to drink it. Guinness is Ireland's national drink and the brewery set up in 1759 by Arthur Guinness (*bottom right*), now fills over four million pints a day and is enshrined in Dublin's architectural history – the philanthropic Guinness family restored **St Patrick's Cathedral**, donated **St Stephen's Green** to the public, cleared slums and replaced them with the **Iveagh Trust** buildings, swimming baths and hostel on Patrick Street.

A visit to the home of Guinness is a high point of any visit to Dublin. The exciting state-of-the-art exhibition, housed in the pint-shaped Guinness Storehouse, explains all about this famous beer. Relax with your pint in the seventh-floor Gravity Bar and enjoy the incredible 360° view of Dublin.

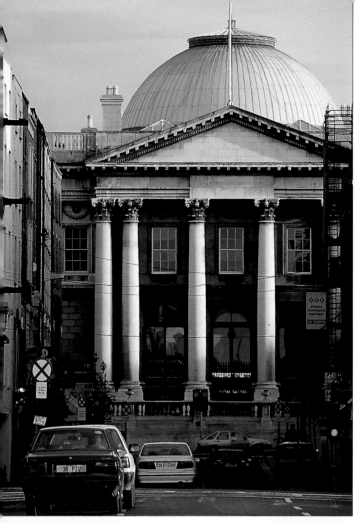

City Hall

Gazing down **Parliament Steet** and across the **Liffey** to **Capel Street** is **City Hall**, once the Royal Exchange. Built between 1769 and 1779 by the Dublin Guild of Merchants, it was turned over to government forces during the 1798 Rebellion for use as an interrogation and torture chamber. Recently restored, it houses the offices of the Dublin City Council and a city museum. In the vaults **The Story of Dublin**, a multi-media exhibition, traces the history of Dublin from 1170. For those in need of refreshment the nearby **Queen of Tarts** café is a popular stop-off point.

College Green and Dame Street

Dame Street leads from **College Green**, just outside the front gates of **Trinity College**, to **City Hall** and on to **Lord Edward Street** and **Christ Church Cathedral**. Outside City Hall it passes the site of Dame Gate, the entrance through the city walls to the medieval town. In the early 18th century, Dame Street was the main street outside the walls of the city and connected the vital centres of power, **Dublin Castle,** which stands behind City Hall, and the **House of Parliament**, now the Bank of Ireland opposite **Trinity College**. The street also contains many buildings in the style known as 'bankers' Georgian' as well as the modern **Central Bank**.

Top left, City Hall faces down Parliament Street toward the River Liffey, bottom left, a view up Dame Street from Trinity College, bottom right, the Rotunda inside City Hall is a stunning and elegant space with its fine domed ceiling and mosaic floor ornamented with the arms of the city. The Latin inscription translates, 'Happy the city where citizens obey'.

Sunlight Chambers

At the corner of Parliament Street and Essex Quay stands one of the most unusual buildings in the city. The **Sunlight Chambers**, built in 1901, was designed as the Irish Headquarters for Lever Brothers, manufacturers of Sunlight soap. The richly ornamented ceramic friezes, in Italian Renaissance style, tell the story of soap, its manufacture and uses.

Dublinia

Life in medieval Dublin (1170-1540) is vividly displayed in the **Dublinia** exhibition, housed in the former Synod Hall at **Christ Church**. The walled city, local laws and customs, the markets and bustle of the streets are depicted through sets and models. Key archaeological finds from the world-famous **Wood Quay** excavation, and other sites, tell the story of both Dublin's élite and her ordinary citizens.

Top, *the Dublinia exhibition is housed in the former Synod Hall (left) and is joined to Christ Church Cathedral (right) by a romantic bridge.*

Bottom, *Boy looking at life-sized reconstruction of a medieval shoemaker at Dublinia.*

Christ Church Cathedral

Christ Church Cathedral stands within the original medieval city walls. Dublin's oldest cathedral, it was founded in 1037 by Sitric Silkenbeard, the king of Viking Dublin. A convert to Christianity he made two pilgrimages to Rome and died, like his father, a monk on the island of Iona off the coast of Scotland. The structure that Silkenbeard had built was made of wood, but over the period 1173 and 1240 the Anglo-Normans rebuilt Silkenbeard's church in stone. This seventy-year long construction period meant that the style of the cathedral encompasses two architectural periods: parts, such as the nave, were built in the Gothic style, while others, among them the **choir** and **transepts**, were built in the Romanesque. A small elongated **head** over the Romanesque doorway in the **south transept** may commemorate either King Henry II of England or Dermot MacMurrough, the King of Leinster responsible for inviting Strongbow, the Earl of Pembroke, and his force of Anglo-Normans into Ireland and thus beginning the long process of colonisation.

By the 19th century the cathedral was in tatters. The whiskey distiller Henry Roe funded a total restoration in 1871 – a mixed blessing as most of the original building was lost and the 14th-century choir was demolished and replaced in mock Romanesque style.

Apart from the medieval **crypt**, Dublin's oldest building, where some of the richly carved stone capitals are preserved, the **transepts** and the north elevation of the **nave**, little of the 13th-century structure remains.

The **crypt** is full of macabre relics. The heart of **St Laurence O'Toole**, the Archbishop of Dublin during the time of Strong-

Top, *Christ Church Cathedral, founded by the Vikings in 1037 and rebuilt by the Anglo-Normans.*

The interior of the cathedral was restored in 1871.

Strongbow's tomb.

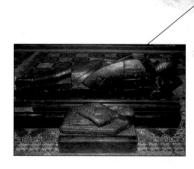

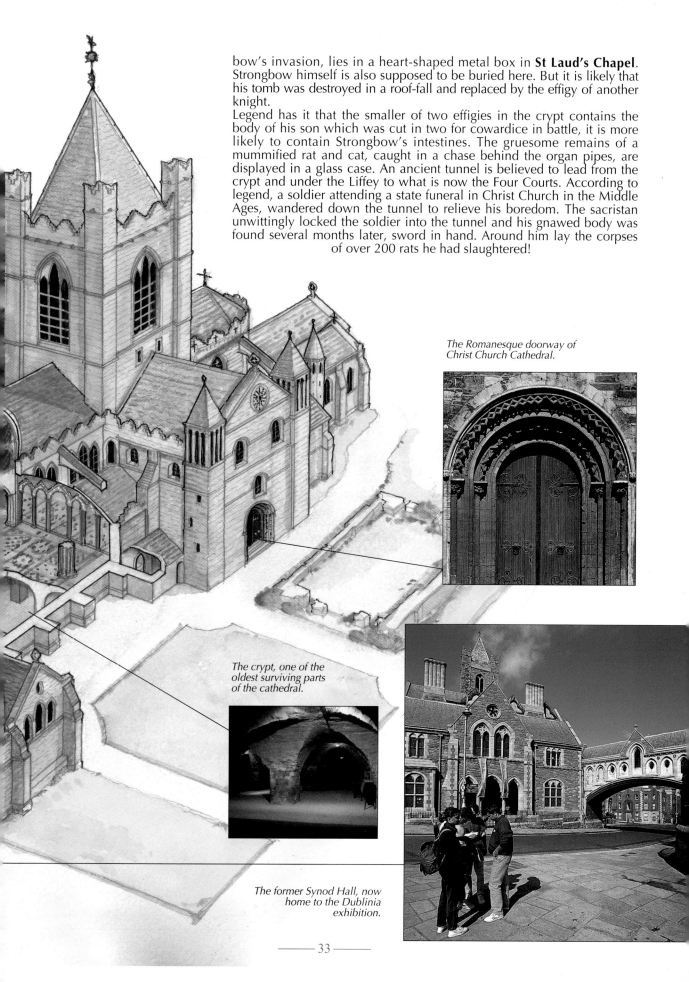

bow's invasion, lies in a heart-shaped metal box in **St Laud's Chapel**. Strongbow himself is also supposed to be buried here. But it is likely that his tomb was destroyed in a roof-fall and replaced by the effigy of another knight.

Legend has it that the smaller of two effigies in the crypt contains the body of his son which was cut in two for cowardice in battle, it is more likely to contain Strongbow's intestines. The gruesome remains of a mummified rat and cat, caught in a chase behind the organ pipes, are displayed in a glass case. An ancient tunnel is believed to lead from the crypt and under the Liffey to what is now the Four Courts. According to legend, a soldier attending a state funeral in Christ Church in the Middle Ages, wandered down the tunnel to relieve his boredom. The sacristan unwittingly locked the soldier into the tunnel and his gnawed body was found several months later, sword in hand. Around him lay the corpses of over 200 rats he had slaughtered!

The Romanesque doorway of Christ Church Cathedral.

The crypt, one of the oldest surviving parts of the cathedral.

The former Synod Hall, now home to the Dublinia exhibition.

St Audoen's Church

Built in 1190 on the remains of an early Christian site dedicated to St Columcille, and named after the Norman St Ouen of Rouen, **St Audoen's** on High Street is the oldest medieval parish church surviving in Dublin. However, the only reminder of its early Christian roots is the gravestone inside the porch known as the 'lucky stone', which is said to bring good fortune to anyone who touches it. The **west doorway** of the original building still survives, while the **bell tower** contains a peal of bells dating from 1423 and said to be the oldest in Ireland. These bells were rung during storms to remind Dubliners to pray for those at sea. The churchyard is bound by a restored section of the old **city walls**, with steps leading down to **St Audoen's Arch**, the only gateway to the old city still standing.

St Audoen's Church and 17ʰ-century bell tower.

Below, *Tower and spike of St Patrick's Cathedral with the Iveagh Trust houses built by Guinness in the foreground.*

Opposite, top, *St Patrick's Park and Cathedral*, opposite, bottom left, *the interior was completely refurbished in 1864.*

St Patrick's Cathedral

Dublin's second Protestant cathedral stands on the oldest Christian site in Dublin, and one believed to be connected with Ireland's patron saint, St Patrick. It suffered a similar history to that of its neighbour Christ Church Cathedral – rebuilt in 1190 in stone in the 'early English' style, it too fell into decay over the centuries. It was also thoroughly restored in 1864 with funds from another drinks merchant, Sir Benjamin Lee Guinness, whose **statue** stands to the right of the entrance. Unlike Christ Church, however, St Patrick's Cathedral stood outside the medieval city walls in the area known as '**the Liberties**' and so became the people's cathedral rather than the place

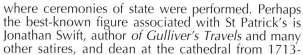

where ceremonies of state were performed. Perhaps the best-known figure associated with St Patrick's is Jonathan Swift, author *of Gulliver's Travels* and many other satires, and dean at the cathedral from 1713-1745. Hugely generous, Swift gave away half his income every year and on his death, the local citizenry pleaded for so many locks of his hair as mementoes that he was buried bald. He is buried in the cathedral beside his beloved Esther Johnson.

Jonathan Swift (1667–1745)

Satirist and political writer, Dublin-born **Jonathan Swift** was the most celebrated dean of St Patrick's Cathedral. In his pamphlets Swift advocated highly controversial views. His most famous work, *Gulliver's Travels,* was published in 1726. Swift's epitaph ends: 'imitate if you can this earnest and dedicated champion of liberty'.

A ceramic disc on a house in Bride Street, depicting a scene from Gulliver's Travels.

Kilmainham Gaol

Built in 1788 in time to house the rebel leaders of the doomed 1798 revolt, this grim prison also held the leaders of the 1916 Rising. The British decided to execute fifteen of the leaders over a number of days. One, James Connolly was so badly wounded that he had to be tied to a chair to face the firing squad. It was one of the worst calculated moves the British had ever made in Ireland and transformed the Rising from a military failure into a romantic gesture that inspired the nationalist cause.

Top, *Kilmainham Gaol where patriots were imprisoned.*

Right, *the serpents above the entrance to Kilmainham Gaol.*

Below, *the former hospital at Kilmainham is now a museum of modern art*, bottom, *Marsh's Library dates from 1701.*

Royal Hospital Kilmainham

Now the **Irish Museum of Modern Art**, the **Royal Hospital Kilmainham** was built in 1680 to house old soldiers and continued to do so until 1922. Inspired by Les Invalides in Paris it was designed by the General Surveyor Sir William Robinson under the direction of the viceroy, the Duke of Ormond. The design is simple and restrained – a colonnaded building with a spire on one side, constructed around a central courtyard. The **hall** and **chapel** interiors are unique – the chapel ceiling is ornamented with relief work of floral and fruit motifs. The hall now hosts classical concerts, while the rest of the museum houses changing collections of Irish and European modern art.

Marsh's Library

The first public library in Ireland was designed in 1701 by Sir William Robinson to house the library of Archbishop Narcissus Marsh. Virtually unchanged since, the library is divided into reading cubicles by Gothic screens which bear the Archbishop's coat of arms. Readers were once kept in the cubicles under lock and key to safeguard the more valuable manuscripts. Over 25,000 books dating from the 16th century onwards are still housed here.

George Bernard Shaw's Birthplace

33 Synge Street, the first home of one of Dublin's winners of the Nobel Prize for Literature, George Bernard Shaw (1856-1950), has been restored and the visitor can step back in time to a Victorian existence.

Right, *George Bernard Shaw's birthplace.*

SOUTH DUBLIN THEATRES

Dublin is noted for its fine theatre performances and is home to many theatres. Built in 1837, the **Gaiety** theatre, on South King Street off Grafton Street, is the oldest theatre in the city. Here productions vary from pantomime to opera.

The old-world Victorian **Olympia** theatre on Dame Street hosts plays, concerts and comedy. Theatregoers are offered a more experimental repertoire in the **Andrew's Lane** theatre, between Grafton Street and Temple Bar. See also p50-1 for theatres in the north of the city.

Left, *inside the Victorian Olympia theatre on Dame Street,* bottom, *the exterior of the theatre.*

PUBS AND NIGHTLIFE

Dubliners say the best **pubs** in the world are to be found in their city. Pubs vary from trendy to traditional. Some of the oldest pubs include **The Palace Bar**, Fleet Street, **Doheny and Nesbitt's**, Lower Baggot Street, **Davy Byrnes**, Duke Street, **O'Neill's**, Suffolk Street and the **Brazen Head**, Lower Bridge Street. Many have live entertainment and an extended licence well into the night. **Temple Bar** is an area of the city which buzzes late at night.

In recent years Dublin has drawn in even more visitors for its nightlife and there is a long list of **nightclubs. Cats** and **The Sugar Club** are to be found on **Lower Leeson Street**. Other well-known nightclubs include **Lillie's Bordello** off **Grafton Street** and **The Pod** on **Harcourt Street**. In summer, those looking for more traditional entertainment can enjoy **Jury's Irish Cabaret**, in Ballsbridge, or Irish Cabaret in the **Burlington Hotel**, Upper Leeson Street.

Brazen Head Pub

Established in 1198, the **Brazen Head** on **Lower Bridge Street** is the oldest pub in Dublin. It has a venerable history – it was also the place where the rebels of the United Irishmen rising of 1798 used to meet to plan their campaign. Nowadays, it plays host to traditional music sessions every night of the week.

Top left, The Brazen Head is Dublin's oldest pub. During summer its courtyard is packed with locals and tourists, while inside, middle, traditional musicians offer entertainment every night.

Left, the Palace Bar, Fleet Street.

Top left, *the Quay's Bar*, top, *The Temple Bar*, left and bottom, *the streets of Temple Bar*.

Temple Bar

The narrow cobbled streets of **Temple Bar** are so full of charm that it is hard to believe that until recently the area was under threat of demolition. Once filled with rundown artists' studios, second-hand clothes shops, printers' warehouses and musty pubs, Temple Bar is now the pride of Dublin City Council with expensive apartments, art galleries, restaurants, nightclubs and the art deco Clarence Hotel owned – and frequented – by U2. But most of all there are its pubs. The pub is central to Irish social life and the best command fierce loyalty and are known far and wide for serving a 'good pint' – a 'pint' often means Guinness. Pulling a *good* pint is an art – and the test of a skilled barman – it takes time and patience and the end result should taste as smooth as velvet.

MUSIC AND DUBLIN

Top, *the evidence of a busy night-empty beer kegs outside the Oliver St John Gogarty Pub.*

From the buskers in **Grafton Street** to the prestigious **National Concert Hall**, on Earlsfort Terrace, close to **St Stephen's Green**, music is never far away in Dublin.

In more recent times international artists like **U2** and **The Cranberries** have put Dublin on the international music map. **Traditional Irish music** has seen a strong revival and can be heard at many of Dublin's pubs, including **O'Donoghue's**, Merrion Row (where the **Dubliners** first preformed), **The Oliver St John Gogarty**, Anglesea Street, and **O'Shea's Merchant Pub**, Bridge Street.

The new Vicar Street pub and music venue reflecting the Augustinian priory church at John's Lane.

Left, *O'Donoghue's pub, Merrion Row, a popular traditional music venue.* Bottom, *the entrance to National Concert Hall.*

Pop concerts are staged at the **Point Theatre**, and other more intimate venues for country, rock, jazz, funk and soul include **Mother Redcap's Tavern**, Back Lane, **Midnight at the Olympia** and **Whelan's** on Wexford Street. **Open-air events** are also common in the summer months and can take place in Temple Bar, St Stephen's Green, Merrion Square, Trinity College and the Phoenix Park and other parks in the suburbs.

Bottom, *the Temple Bar Blues Festival.*

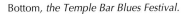

The Liffey

It is because of the River Liffey and its many tributaries that Dublin has more than one name.

In Irish it is *Baile Átha Cliath* or 'town of the hurdle ford' – the ford dated from before the Vikings and resembled a causeway that spanned the river, which in those days was very wide and shallow. Then there is the city's English name, *Dubh Linn* or 'Black Pool', named after the pool of water formed by the Poddle river as it joined the Liffey near Dublin Castle.

To complicate matters further, the section of Liffey passing through the city also had a name – *Ruirthech* or 'Turbulent River'. Just how turbulent it was can be judged from an entry in the ancient *Annals* which records that in 770AD an entire Ulster army drowned as it attempted to wade across. Now, the Liffey is better behaved and, constrained between the quays, it runs quietly out into the sea at Ringsend, dividing Dublin neatly into two – the southside with its chic shopping streets, expensive restaurants, pubs and nightclubs and the northside where James Gandon's splendid public buildings are surrounded by a rapidly changing city.

O'Connell Bridge

Designed by James Gandon in 1790 to link the south side of Dublin to the north, the bridge is roughly as broad as it is long and continues north up **O'Connell Street**, Dublin's main thoroughfare.

Below, *view of the River Liffey,* opposite, top right, *view north from O'Connell Bridge,* opposite, bottom right, *O'Connell Bridge at sunset.*

The Spire and the Boardwalk

The area just north of the **Liffey** is rapidly evolving and there are exciting plans for the future, including wider granite-paved footpaths, the **Luas** tram system and clipped lime and plane trees planted to create a boulevard on **O'Connell Street**.

The Spire of Dublin

Ian Ritchie's **Monument of Light** was the winning entry in Dublin's millennium design competition for a new monument in **O'Connell Street**. Rising 120 metres high and made of stainless steel, Dublin's **Spire** is the tallest sculpture in the world. The Spire is 3 metres wide at the base and 15 centimetres in diameter at the apex. At night, white light flows from the 11,650 perforations at the top of the monument; by day sunlight and reflections bounce off the surface of this imposing structure.

The Boardwalk

From O'Connell Street, the **Boardwalk** offers a pleasant stroll down the north bank of the **Liffey**. There are seats and cafés along the way where the visitor can enjoy the reflection of the bridges and buildings on the water.

General Post Office

The **General Post Office** (GPO) is the most significant building on **O' Connell Street**, not so much for its architectural merit as for its place in Irish history. On Easter Monday 1916 a small band of rebels made it

Left, *the old and the new, the General Post Office and the Spire,* bottom, *the Boardwalk.*

their headquarters and their poet leader, Patrick Pearse, stood outside to read the Proclamation of the Irish Republic to the few disinterested passersby. A week of shelling by British troops followed, leaving the GPO and most of **Lower O'Connell Street** gutted. The rebels evacuated to **Moore Street** and surrendered soon after. It was a disastrous military defeat.

But from then on, Irish independence became just a matter of time. In the Civil War of 1922 O'Connell Street again suffered and only the façade of the GPO remained. Now beautifully restored and a working post office it houses a statue of '*The Fall of Cúchulainn*', the mythic Ulster hero, to commemorate the 1916 Rising.

Top, *the elegant Ha'penny Bridge,*
bottom right, *the Lír clock, a Dublin landmark.*

VIKING TOUR OF DUBLIN

Viking Splash is a popular and fun tour of Dublin by land and water, in a reconditioned Second-World-War, amphibious vehicle (a 'Duck'). The costumed captain relates how the Vikings left their mark on the city, and the participants, in their Viking helmets, learn the Viking roar! The tour concludes with a splash into the historic **Grand Canal Basin**.

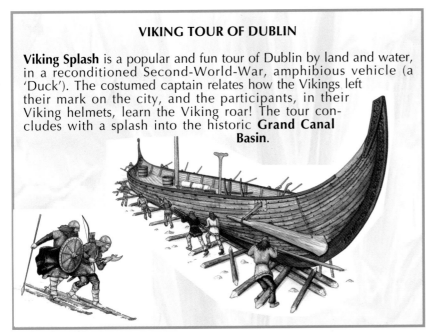

O'Connell Street

O'Connell Street is called after Daniel O'Connell (1775-1847), 'The Liberator', who campaigned for the Act of Catholic Emancipation (1829). Designed by John Henry Foley, his fine statue stands at the **O'Connell Bridge** end of the street. The Winged Victories around the base represent Patriotism, Fidelity, Courage and Eloquence. Along the central mall are many statues, including: the founder of Ireland's Trade Union Movement, 'Big Jim', James Larkin (1876-1947); the Capuchin Father Mathew (1790-1856), champion of the temperance movement; on the central island where **Parnell Street** crosses the top of **O'Connell Street**, Charles Stewart Parnell (1846-1891), president of the Irish National Land League and supporter of Home Rule, surveys the city.

Around O'Connell Street

Henry Moore, Earl of Drogheda, originally planned the area around O'Connell Street. His desire for immortality led him to commemorate his entire title in their names – **Henry Street**, **Moore Street, Earl Street**, **Of Lane** and **Drogheda Street** (now the top of O'Connell Street). Henry and Moore streets are busy shopping areas, with department stores and shopping centres offering the best bargains in town. Moore Street is famous for the ranks of street-traders advertising their wares in singsong Dublin accents.

Top, *the Moore Street market,* bottom right, *Clery's department store, O'Connell Street.*
Opposite, top, *the interior of St Mary's Pro-Cathedral, Marlborough Street, parallel to O'Connell Street,* and opposite, bottom, *James Joyce's statue, North Earl Street.*

Shopping and Cinema

The area north of the **Liffey** offers fine shopping streets, including **O'Connell Street**, **Henry Street**, **Mary Street**, and the colourful flower and fruit stalls of **Moore Street**. **O'Connell Street** is home to the long-established **Clery's** department store and across the road is one of the city's biggest bookshops, **Easons**. **Henry Street** is a busy pedestrianised shopping street and here **Arnotts'** large department store opened its doors one hundred years ago. Dublin has many **cinemas** – some south of the river such as the **Irish Film Centre** in **Temple Bar**. On the northside, the **UGC Parnell Centre** offers ten screens and the **Savoy** on O' Connell Street has a good choice of programmes.

James Joyce (1882–1941)

Considered by some to be the greatest writer, in English, of the 20th century, Dublin-born **James Joyce** went into self-imposed exile from Ireland in 1904. Alongside his famous work, *Ulysses* (1922), his other writings include *Dubliners* (1914), a volume of short stories, the semiauto-biographical *A Portrait of the Artist as a Young Man* (1916) and the experimental *Finnegans Wake* (1939). Joyce died in Zurich.

The James Joyce Museum, Sandycove tower.

National Botanic Gardens

The **National Botanic Gardens** in Glasnevin, to the north of the city, were founded in 1795. Covering 48 acres by the River Tolka, the gardens are home to an arboretum, a bog garden and a Burren area among other features. Famous for their **glasshouses**, including the beautifully restored Curvilinear Range, designed and built by Richard Turner between 1843 and 1869, the gardens also contain **The Great Palm House**, built in 1884, and an orchid house. Among the 20,000 species of plants are a fine weeping Atlantic cedar, Chusan palms, and strawberry trees.

Opposite, top left, the James Joyce Cultural Centre, North Great Georges Street, opposite, right, James Joyce's statue and the Spire.

This page, right, Glasnevin Cemetery, bottom, the National Botanic Gardens.

Glasnevin Cemetery

Close to the **National Botanic Gardens** is **Glasnevin Cemetery**. Opened in 1831 to give Catholics a place of burial, the 124 acres of this cemetery now contain the remains of over one million people. Threatened by grave robbers, walls and towers were built to protect the cemetery in 1845. The graves reflect Dublin's social, political and cultural history over the past one hundred and seventy years. A round tower rises from the grave of Daniel O'Connell. Among the famous buried here are Charles Stewart Parnell, Eamon de Valera, Brendan Behan, Maud Gonne and Michael Collins. The free guided tour on Wednesday and Friday afternoons is one of the best in Dublin.

Hugh Lane
Municipal Gallery of Modern Art

Located on **Parnell Square**, at the north end of O'Connell Street, this art museum was once the town-house of the Earl of Charlemont, appropriately enough a patron of the arts. It was designed by Sir William Chambers in 1762 in the days when the rich and powerful lived north of the Liffey and is one of the pleasantest galleries in Dublin to browse in because of its compact size. Its collection of 19th- and 20th-century European art includes Impressionist works collected by Sir Hugh Lane, an art dealer who bequeathed his collection to Dublin Corporation in 1908. After his death aboard the torpedoed *Lusitania* in 1915, a legal battle raged between Dublin and London as to who should own the collection. It has only recently been resolved and the pictures are now shared by the Tate Gallery in London and the Hugh Lane.

Gate and Abbey Theatres

The **Abbey** is one of the great names in world theatre. Founded by William Butler Yeats and Lady Augusta Gregory in 1904, its aims were to present Irish dramatic lit-

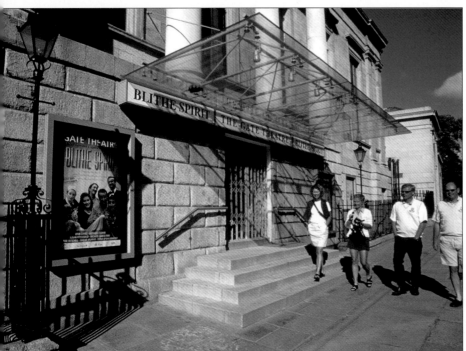

Opposite, top left, *the Hugh Lane Municipal Gallery of Modern Art on Parnell Square, with Oisín Kelly's statue of The Children of Lír, in the Garden of Remembrance,* bottom left, *the façade of the Gate Theatre, on Parnell Square,* bottom right, *the famous Abbey Theatre.*

Top, *in the Dublin Writers' Museum, built in the heyday of Georgian Dublin, the elegant Gallery of Writers is decorated with elaborate stucco work.*

erature. The present theatre opened in 1966 and is located in Lower Abbey Street off O'Connell Street. The smaller **Peacock** theatre is in the same complex. The **Gate** theatre, on Parnell Square, won international fame under the direction of Micheál MacLiammóir and Hilton Edwards. Plays by Oscar Wilde, George Bernard Shaw and Samuel Beckett are often produced here.

Dublin Writers' Museum

A few doors away from the Hugh Lane Gallery, at **Nos 18** and **19 Parnell Square**, are the **Dublin Writers' Museum** and **Irish Writers' Centre** respectively. Ireland is known for its writers – four have received the Nobel Prize for Literature, William Butler Yeats, George Bernard Shaw, Samuel Beckett and Seamus Heaney, and their work and lives, and that of many other famous writers, are covered here.

Parnell Square

Construction began on **Parnell Square** in the 1750s. By the 1780s it boasted more peers, politicians and bishops among its residents than any other street in Dublin. The square was originally named Rutland Square after the viceroy of the period, but it was later renamed in memory of the nationalist leader, Charles Stewart Parnell, whose statue stands at the top of O'Connell Street. The centre of the square used to contain the Pleasure Gardens, a fundraising venture in the 1740s by Dr Bartholomew Mosse, the barber-surgeon who used the entrance fees from patrons to finance the building of the Lying-in (Rotunda) Hospital on the south side of Parnell Square. It was the first maternity hospital in Europe and is still in use. All that now remains of the Gardens is a small square of green on the north side of Parnell Square, opposite the **Dublin Writers' Museum**, called the **Garden of Remembrance** which commemorates the 1916 Rising.

Custom House

In 1779 architect James Gandon turned down an offer to work in St Petersburg. Instead he came to Dublin to work on what would become one of the finest examples of Georgian building in Europe. Gandon remained in Ireland for the rest of his life, contributing two more splendid public buildings to Dublin's architecture – the **Four Courts** and **King's Inns**.

Begun in 1781 and costing £400,000 over ten years, the Custom House was not an easy project – the site was sea-sodden and required constant draining and elaborate foundations to prevent subsidence, workmen demanded constant wage increases, the enemies of the project hired mobs to vandalise the construction and Gandon found it wise to wear his sword whenever he visited. But none of these obstacles nor a fire nor even the death of his wife deterred Gandon, and in 1791 the Custom House, built of gleaming Portland stone, was finished.

The **south front** with its graceful Corinthian portico flanked by arcades faces onto the river, while the **north front** faces onto what remains of the Georgian Gardiner Street. The fourteen **Riverine Heads** over the doors and windows, depicting the main rivers of Ireland, and the figure of **Commerce** on the dome are by the sculptor Edward Smyth, Gandon's discovery who, he declared, was the equal of Michelangelo.

In 1921 the Custom House was targeted by nationalist forces. A fire raged for days melting down brass fittings and causing cracks in the stonework. Restored in 1926, the drum of the dome was replaced by Irish Ardbraccan stone rather than the white Portland stone of the original and it has aged badly. By the 1970s more major renovations were necessary and the present Custom House was unveiled in 1991.

Top left, *the south front of the Custom House built by James Gandon*, bottom, left, *behind the recently built International Financial Services Centre.*

Top, *the Four Courts by James Gandon is a masterpiece of Georgian Dublin*, bottom right, *St Michan's Church founded in 1096 by the Vikings and known for the mummified bodies that are preserved here.*

Four Courts

The second of James Gandon's landmark Georgian buildings, the **Four Courts** was commissioned by the Duke of Rutland in 1796 to replace the decaying courts near Christ Church. It contains several Gandon flourishes – facing onto the river with a central Corinthian portico and side wings connected by arcades, with sculptural work by Edward Smyth.

St Michan's Church

Only the tower now survives of the church founded by the Vikings in 1096 and for centuries the only parish church north of the Liffey. The interior is plain but contains an organ on which Handel is believed to have played while composing *The Messiah*. But St Michan's is best known for the mummified bodies that are preserved in its 17th-century vaults. Outside in the graveyard, drawn perhaps by the macabre corpses in the vaults, Bram Stoker, the author of *Dracula*, used to pace.

Top, *the gracious façade of King's Inns, James Gandon's last public building.*

King's Inns

Designed in 1786, the **King's Inns** was the last of James Gandon's great public buildings and still serves its original function of providing training and facilities for barristers. While the foundation stone was laid by the Earl of Clare in 1795, construction did not begin until 1802. Gandon had left Ireland in 1797, suspecting rightly that the city was on the point of revolution. When he returned after the 1798 rebellion he faced a backlog of work. He was nearly sixty years of age by this time and suffering acutely from gout and so he passed the bulk of the work on the King's Inns to his protegée Henry Aaron Baker. The building was finally completed in 1817, by which time Gandon had long since retired to his house in north Dublin.

Like the Four Courts and the Custom House the King's Inns was designed to front onto water – a branch of the Royal Canal once extended past here. A graceful **cupola** rises over the central archway. On the left a doorway leads to the dining room – Irish barristers must consume a set number of dinners per year. On either side of the doorway are two female **caryatides** by Edward Smyth, the sculptor favoured by James Gandon. On the left is Cares, goddess of food, while on the right stands a follower of Bacchus holding a wine goblet. The figures flanking the doorway to the right of the central archway are more sober. This is the doorway to the former prerogative court, now the Registry of Deeds, and the figures represent 'Law', carrying a book and a quill, and 'Security' with a key and scroll.

Smithfield

The old horse and cattle market in the north of the city has been transformed into a pedestrianised **piazza** – the largest open public space in the city centre. Twelve steel masts with their braziers and sails illuminate the cobbled square at night. For stunning views of Dublin, the visitor can take a glass lift up the **Chimney Observation Tower**, a platform perched on top of the former **Jameson Distillery Chimney** (56.4 metres high). A tour of the **Old Jameson Distillery** whiskey centre comes highly recommended and the piazza offers a variety of shops and restaurants, the **Ceol Irish Traditional Music Centre** and Chief O'Neill's Hotel and Bar.

The Old Jameson Distillery

Just north of the Liffey in **Smithfield Village** lies the **Old Jameson Distillery**. Now a visitor centre, the tour explains the history, manufacture and unique taste of Irish whiskey or *uisce beatha* (pronounced 'ishke baha') in Irish; this translates as the 'water of life'. The tour concludes with the popular whiskey-tasting session. For an additional fascinating insight into the techniques and traditions of brewing, the **Dublin Brewing Company** on North King Street, also in Smithfield, is one of Dublin's finest craft breweries.

Top, *Smithfield with the Chimney Observation Tower* and above, *the Old Jameson Distillery,* bottom right, *Collins Barracks, founded in 1702.*

The National Museum of Decorative Arts and History, Collins Barracks

Founded in 1702, **Collins Barracks** was the oldest occupied military barracks in Europe until refurbished in 1997 for the National Museum of Ireland. Now the **National Museum of Decorative Arts and History**, the building fronts onto the River Liffey at Benburb Street. The museum charts Ireland's economic, social, political and military progress through the centuries. An impressive exhibition of **Irish Silver** traces the silversmith's craft from the 17th century to the present day. The **Irish Period Furniture** exhibition, including pieces by Eileen Gray, displays furniture from 1690 to the 20th century. A series of galleries houses folklife artefacts, giving an insight into the crafts, cultures and traditions of the Irish people.

DUBLIN'S CANALS AND THE PHOENIX PARK

Top, *a quiet stretch of the Grand Canal.*

Left, *'O commemorate me where there is water,*
Canal water preferably, so stilly
Greeny at the heart of summer ...'
from Lines Written on a Seat on the Grand Canal, Dublin *by*
poet Patrick Kavanagh (1904-1967).

Dublin's Canals

In 1715 an act of parliament proposed a canal link between Dublin and the rivers Shannon in the west and Barrow in the south. As a result two canals were built – the **Royal Canal** on the northside of Dublin, and the **Grand Canal** which met the Liffey at Ringsend, cut south of the city past **Portobello** and **Dolphin's Barn** where there was a harbour, and led eventually to the Shannon. However, once the railways were firmly established these waterways were no longer competitive, and commercial traffic stopped in the 1960s. Since then the canals have been left to those who enjoy walking along its grassy towpath.

Phoenix Park

The **Phoenix Park,** in the north west of the city, is one of the largest enclosed parks in the world and covers 1,752 acres. In 1662, the Duke of Ormond stocked the park with fallow deer and partridge. Opened to the public in 1747 by Lord Chesterfield, the park's name came from the Irish *fionn uisce,* meaning a clear-water spring, not the mythical bird. This beautiful park contains many items of interest, including: the 63-metre-tall **Wellington Monument,** built to commemorate the Dublin-born Duke of Wellington, victor at The Battle of Waterloo (1815); the **Papal Cross,** erected to mark the visit of Pope John Paul II (1979); **Áras an Uachtaráin**, the residence of the President of Ireland; the 17th-century **Ashtown Castle**; a visitors' centre and café; with over 700 different animals, **Dublin Zoo** is famous for breeding lions, and produced the roaring MGM lion. Giraffes, rhinos, zebra and hippos roam freely on the **African Plains**, a savannah for some of the Zoo's largest residents.

Garden of Remembrance, Islandbridge

Nearly 150,000 Irishmen fought in the First World War, and the 50,000 who died are commemorated by the Sir Edward Lutyens' memorial in the **Garden of Remembrance at Islandbridge.**

Farmleigh

Farmleigh is situated in the northwest corner of the **Phoenix Park**. The main house is a fine example of Georgian-Victorian architecture. This mansion (which formally belonged to the Guinness family) stands on 79 acres, and contains a Sunken Garden, a Walled Garden, the famous Clock Tower and a lake with a classical fountain. Farmleigh provides accommodation for visiting dignitaries and hosts important international meetings.

Top, middle right, and bottom, *scenes from Dublin Zoo in the Phoenix Park,* middle left, *Garden of Remembrance.*

SPORT AND DUBLIN

Dublin has much to offer the sporting enthusiast. From the skilful speed of **gaelic football** and the ancient Irish stick-and-ball game of **hurling** at **Croke Park,** headquarters of the GAA (Gaelic Athletic Association, 1884), to the cut and thrust of international and national **rugby** and **soccer** at **Lansdowne Road,** in Ballsbridge. **Golf** is Ireland's fastest growing sport and there are over 50 courses to choose from within an hour of the city, among them the **K Club**, in County Kildare and the **Portmarnock Golf Links,** just 25 minutes north of the city. For those who love horses, there are racecourses at **Leopardstown**, south Dublin, **Fairyhouse**, County Meath, and the **Curragh**, County Kildare. The fast and furious sport of **polo** can be wit-

nessed in the **Phoenix Park**. Or you can ride out yourself from the many equestrian centres around the city. **Greyhound racing** takes place at **Harold's Cross Park**, near Rathmines, and at **Shelbourne Park** at Ringsend.

Hemmed in by the sea, it is no surprise that water sports such as **sailing**, **windsurfing** and **swimming** are ever popular. Dublin Bay offers yacht clubs in **Dun Laoghaire**, **Howth**, **Malahide** and **Clontarf**. Windsurfing is popular in the **Monkstown** area, south of the city. For swimming, there are sandy beaches at **Killiney**, south Dublin, and **Donabate** in the north; other swimming areas are the **Forty Foot** in **Sandycove**, and **Seapoint** to the south. The water in the Irish Sea always remains chilly and refuge can be taken in a number of indoor swimming pools!

Opposite, top, *sailing from Howth*, bottom, *a view of Howth's golf course*, and this page, top right, *horse riding*, middle, *rugby at Lansdowne Road*, bottom right, *hurling at Croke Park*.

AROUND DUBLIN

Dublin sits in a magnificent bay which stretches south to Killiney and north to the tiny fishing port of Howth. Bronze Age sites, historic castles and abbeys and sublime views as well as associations with famous writers, poets and painters make the Dublin coastline one well worth exploring. South of Dublin, the Victorian seaside town of **Dun Laoghaire** is the yachting centre of the east coast. It has four yachtclubs and a fine harbour bound by two mile-long stone piers which point out into Dublin Bay. In the long summer evenings the piers are thronged with Dubliners watching the racing yachts vie for space around the race marks. A mile or so south of **Dun Laoghaire** in **Sandycove**, a **Martello Tower** stands on the edge of the shoreline, one of a string of twenty-five coastal defensive structures built in anticipation of an invasion by Napoleon. None of them ever saw action and they have been converted into shops, homes, museums or left to crumble. The Sandycove tower now houses memorabilia of Ireland's most famous exile, James Joyce, who once spent a few days here.

His friend, the Dublin surgeon, writer and wit Oliver St John Gogarty, owned the tower and sometimes stayed there to write his poetry. In 1904, Joyce joined him. A few days later, however, they quarrelled and Joyce moved out. Gogarty said he would have thrown him out sooner but for his fear that if Joyce 'made a name someday' it would be remembered against him. His fears came true. When Joyce came to write *Ulysses*, he set the opening scenes in the tower, with 'stately, plump' Buck Mulligan carrying out his daily ablutions. Gogarty was the model for Buck Mulligan and he was not pleased with the honour Joyce paid him. On one side of the tower is a rocky bathing place known as the **Forty Foot**, not for its depth but because the 40th Regiment of Foot of the British army was stationed here. It used to be the preserve of men only who delighted in 'skinny-dipping', but female liberation has come to the Forty Foot and now the swimmers – both male and female – are more modestly dressed. These toughened bathers brave the icy waters of the Irish Sea all year round.

The broad stretch of Killiney Bay.

Sandycove, with the Martello Tower which houses the James Joyce Museum, to the right of it is the white block of architect Michael Scott's house built in the 1930s.

Further south along the coast is **Dalkey,** once a medieval walled town and important trading post. The town has captured the imagination of several writers – Flann O'Brien (Brian Nolan), the brilliant satirical novelist, used it in *The Dalkey Archives*, while playwright Hugh Leonard set his play *Da* there. In recent years, Dalkey has become the Beverly Hills of Ireland with the beautiful houses tucked away behind high walls or chipped out of the Dalkey hillside and owned by musicians such as Bono from U2 and Chris de Burgh, writer Maeve Binchy, or film directors like Neil Jordan. But for all that the atmosphere of Dalkey has not changed. It is still a charming place to ramble or sit and watch for stars. Behind the village is Dalkey Hill, its disused quarry leaving a scarred cliff-face. A ridge leads from the quarry to a public park on **Killiney Hill** and offers breathtaking views of Dublin Bay and inland to the Wicklow mountains.

A short distance to the seaward side of Dalkey village is tiny **Coliemore Harbour**, packed with fishing boats, nets and tackle. Boats go from here to **Dalkey Island** a rocky, windswept island off **Sorrento Point**. Perched on one end of this little island is another **Martello Tower**, as well as a ruined early Christian church dedicated to **St Begnet**.

Top, *view along the coast of Sandycove and Killiney Bay,*
left, *Powerscourt House and Gardens, Enniskerry.*

One of the most popular excursions to the south of the city is **Powerscourt House, Gardens and Waterfall**, Enniskerry, County Wicklow. The 18th-century Palladian house has been restored, is open to the public and offers a designer-shopping experience, fine cafés and a golf course. The views of Wicklow from the avenue, and from the restaurant, are simply stunning. The stylish, Italian-inspired gardens blend in with this sublime setting, and the waterfall, Ireland's tallest cascade, is a popular picnic spot a few kilometres away.

On the northernmost tip of Dublin Bay is **Howth Head** which comes to a point at the Baily lighthouse.

Together with **Dalkey Island** on the southernmost tip, it curves round to form the sheltered harbour of Dublin Bay. Its height and commanding views across the bay and, on a clear day, across the Irish Sea to Wales, gave it military importance from the earliest times and wave after wave of invaders have left their mark here. According to legend a cairn on top of Howth Head marks the grave of an early Celtic chieftain. Centuries later Viking raiders must have realised how perfect a site this was as they nosed along the coast looking for somewhere to set up a trading post. They left evidence of their time here in the ruined **Howth Abbey** which Sigtrygg, the Norse king of Dublin, founded in 1042. Inside lies the tomb of Christian St Lawrence and his wife, ancestors of the Normans, the next wave of conquerors to come to Ireland. Hundreds of years later, the St Lawrence family still lives in **Howth Castle.**

On the northside of the head is **Howth Harbour**, once an important port but now flourishing with the new marina and yachtclub. Fishing boats go out from the harbour, circling round **Ireland's Eye**, the tiny island almost in the mouth of the harbour, to reach the open sea. On the island is another **Martello Tower**, as well as the remains of the 6th-century monastic settlement of **St Nessan**. But these days it is uninhabited except for the many birds who take sanctuary there.

Looking towards Dublin city from Howth, long stretches of sand and dunes catch the eye. These are the protected areas of **Dollymount Strand**, packed with Dubliners on warm summer days, and **Bull Island** – a sandy spit, topped by grassy dunes and joined by a wooden bridge to shore. In winter, the only visitors here are the thousands of birds who use this as a stop-off point.

North of Howth lies **Malahide Castle**, home to the Talbot family from 1185 to 1973. Set in 250 acres of parkland, this romantic castle is a blend of many architectural styles and houses fine period furniture, a collection of Irish portrait paintings and a resident ghost.

Top right, *the coast near Howth Head, at the north of Dublin Bay,* middle, *Howth Abbey founded by the Norse in 1042 with, in the distance, the harbour and Ireland's Eye, a bird sanctuary,* bottom, *Malahide Castle.*

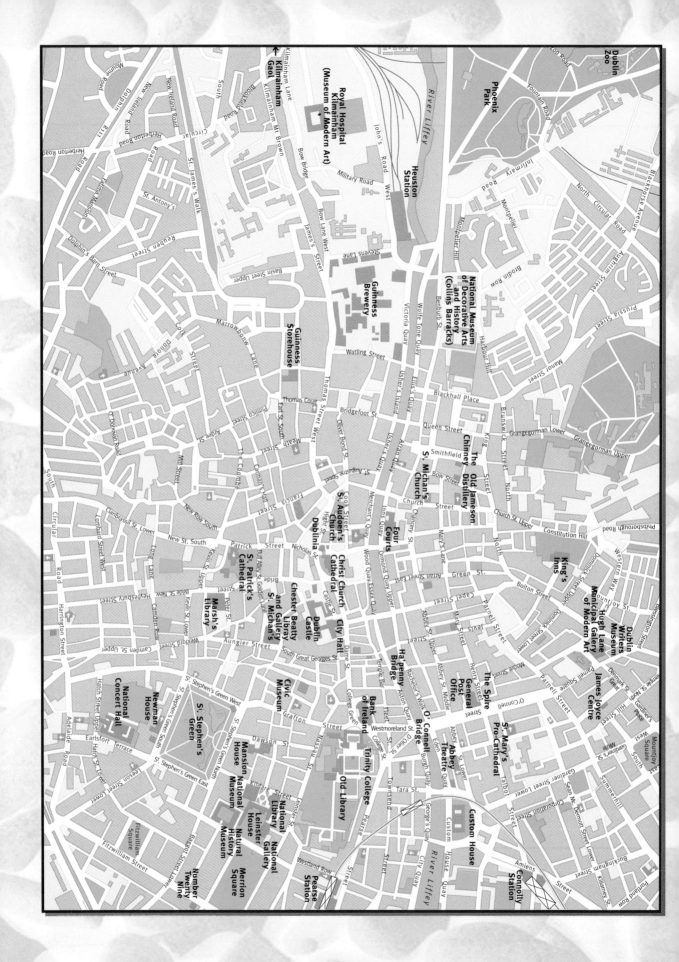